WHAT IF THE INVADER IS BEAUTIFUL

Also by Louise Mathias

The Traps
Lark Apprentice

WHAT IF THE INVADER IS BEAUTIFUL

Louise Mathias

Four Way Books
Tribeca

Library of Congress Cataloging-in-Publication Data

Names: Mathias, Louise, 1975- author.
Title: What if the invader is beautiful / Louise Mathias.
Other titles: What if the invader is beautiful (Compilation)
Description: New York : Four Way Books, 2024.
Identifiers: LCCN 2024000673 (print) | LCCN 2024000674 (ebook) | ISBN
9781961897083 (trade paperback) | ISBN 9781961897090 (epub)
Subjects: LCGFT: Poetry.
Classification: LCC PS3613.A828 W47 2024 (print) | LCC PS3613.A828
(ebook) | DDC 811/.6--dc23/eng/20240116
LC record available at https://lccn.loc.gov/2024000673
LC ebook record available at https://lccn.loc.gov/2024000674

This book is manufactured in the United States of America and printed on
acid-free paper.

Four Way Books is a not-for-profit literary press. We are grateful for the assistance
we receive from individual donors, public arts agencies, and private foundations
including the New York State Council on the Arts, a state agency.

PROUD MEMBER

We are a proud member of the Community of Literary Magazines and Presses.

Contents

THREE

For Jeff Griffin, whose moonlit kindness saved me

ONE

(I thought of you,
collapsing like a hymn.)

Three Types of Mimicry

I pictured butterflies each time the boy was hurting me.
I say *boy*, though he was north of forty. I say *hurt*, because for years
I spoke in pretty code. There are no butterflies on Mars,

and here on earth, *Mohavea*
confertiflora dupes the bees because she has to—
as when I told the boy he made me come

because the other path was frozen lakes and crosshairs.
What color are my eyes? I asked his back,
a dense arithmetic of bramble, fear and birdsong.

In the Poem No One Knows is about Me, I'm Pretty Much Prey

Nightjars depend on their cryptic coloration.
Almost, he said, like a blonde

peeing in a field of goldenrod.

What's a leg when you're caught in a trap?
Moonflowers shriek from the side of the road.

Lord, let me die

in a godforsaken town,
not even the air

to notice.

Doomsway

More strange than the way music matters,
is the fact that these flowers rage on

pursuing of storm, long after

the split ends of summer, rosy boas
can mate all day—

hearts growing larger with conjure.

Some say the tree seduced the axe.
My anger he said

looking right in my face
is global.

Dom

In a country where roses grew well, I lost it all.
My will to be

his glittering acquisition. What stars are for.

Dopamine/synapse,
history/fail.

Some day, I'll call this what it is.
Shame is a dove

her soft side
filled with maggots.

Before We Became a Danger to Each Other

There was a violence under elms and
under oaks.

His hands around my throat

until I blurted *cliffrose*. No word
is ever safe, said every wind born westerly.

And then we were thrown,
each other's most inclement weather.

Real Country Dark

Everything hurts in the half-light.
In the fields, I was told I was childish

in a field of fragrant bells,
blood

dripped seductive down on my leg.
Ever been helpless at night-lake?

Must be like dying, I thought,
the road a hopeless tunnel

veering left.

Lavic

In mineral environs, he told me not to breathe.
I thought of you, collapsing

like a hymn. Beyond

the ravening rocks
with a death wish imbedded—

What kind of a landscape *does* that?
And the darker plains

are always called Maria. Sea of Moon.

What holds me
in this parliament of rage?

Fathoms

Maybe to touch it, gently to the throat.
Some flowers have throats

where do they think they are going?

**

Red cave
of the mouth.

Warm pet
of the mouth

To persist in her
(an address).

**

Dragging me across like a star—

If, as Borges said
the magic is severe

**

Act like a human,
my once-husband said.

We were standing
in our very own shitty kitchen.

My animal smelling your animal
across eight states.

**

To speak of feed and flowers
Or her muzzle and her fur.

(She can incorporate all hunters.)

**

Destroyer of mornings,
destroy.

Some years ago now,
some eyes.

Some eyes that obliterate trains.

Black Ice

Less sure of my footing now,
which had always been the grim attendant.

The darker child in him I thought was mine.
You can form the word in your mouth, you can utter it even
but nothing is ever, whatever, his curious vowels.

Who puts a gun inside a tulip? Feeds a spider another spider?

I'm not saying his eyes were not oceans.
I'm saying those oceans were knives.

Searchlight

Talking to him
was like trying to fuck a cloud.

So I drove on the spare
'til the gas ran out.

Still sounds like a threat
when I touch it.

Stole

No longer embroidered
with my previous owner's initials.

Who bleats for me, inside his omened sleep—
whose small emergency grows.

In the hills behind the DMV, two
ponies fucking in the lupine.

I know you know I paid my fee.
I'm nobody's pony now.

The Violets Have a Backup Plan

Purple-thief-of-the-gospels adorn the road
the blood-fed ranch.

Lilies
and their allies.

American Lady, Painted Lady, West Coast Lady.

He asked you to decorate hell and
you fell for it. Viola of the stream, the bog,

viola of—

Forgiveness comes when I say it does,
and with a sever.

Eidolon

Washed my hair
in the kitchen sink. Humans

hadn't seen me in a while. This was the fall
into Spring

when I would not

listen to music.
Music like vapor from horses,
it could not exist.

Vapor from horses,
now playing in room #9—

Almost I think that I loved him
the way he took photos,
I didn't seem there.

Another

mauled river
I did not snap
my neck in.

Last Chance Range

Vexed light on dune evening primrose.

The mineral lands denuded,
this still hurts.

Did I leave or was I left, slowly.
Last of the summer's

nectar on the blade.

Here, where the sand makes songs when
the wind directs her—

And the singing is an irritant
made eerie.

TWO

*(No language
ever loved me back.)*

The Problem of Hands

And how to fill them
is the problem of cigarettes and paint.

First time I felt my undoing
was in front of

a painting—Sam Francis, I believe.

Oh, his bloomed out, Xanax-ed California.

I liked the word *guard*, but you know

we made each other
nervous, standing too close

for everyone concerned. All art being

a form of violence
as a peony
is violence.

Here you come

with your open hands.

Delves

A small bridge leads to the sea,
but you do not cross it.

No guide, no bottle,
no bible, no gun.

Just the softest of wars
between wind &

some kind of sister poppy—

Ant in the golden
forest of your hair, finds the good place

to die, at last.
And the light does not exhaust

admiring him.

Lorazepam

Our contract was balletic—
you took from me

the rabbits spooked
inside their still-damp nest.

Then you were a room I lived through,
entirely. Snowed in

all the way up to my guilt.

"One form of heaven is nothing."

Ignorable now, the gnaw
a highway's plaintive hiss.

Mecca

He comes to me with something on his hands neither one of us can identify. I quit trying and the orchid drops her blossoms to the floor. Discarded little skirts. It's 108, too hot for blindfolds, problems not involving blood. *City of Anna*, he mumbles. Your neck as a golden distributor of sweat. Two shadows, all-fours. Smoothing the motel bedspread like this were a church. Like all chemicals, I bloomed in secret, for a while.

Spy Mountain

He calls me at midnight to talk about "the bloom." How mostly I hid in the folds there. Once, when we were done, there was blood on the front of my shirt. I liked that he didn't ignore it. Within fifteen minutes, the roses I stole near the Wasco State Prison were irredeemably wilted. Everyone knows a woman's body can incorporate the dead. *Hello?* I say, then retreat into codes the color of veins apparent. Turns out, the shed skin is much longer than the snake. I kept on blooming while he watched.

Bombay Beach

You know someone, somewhere.
A collection of knives, linoleum, unfortunately.

There's a room now in the chest,
comprised of a secretive clock—

clock in, clock out. The blonde

unfastens the strap,
sorry human noise

divorced
of song, unlatched now in the palms,

cocaine and ridicule,
but also, love, also.

Sylvan Instance

Come over.
Help me bury that

where-do-I-bury-the-body look.

And the bullshit tree I was born in.
While your eyes were closed, it snowed, but only vaguely.

Reminds me of a breast a friend described,
so white it held the world up for a time.

This drag I take to stave off loss.
It's winter now, your hair the color of cornfields

behind my childhood house
where we all rehearsed our cruelty.

And the Eastern Sierra hills
where I slipped

out of the rope that held me.

Girl wrapped round a steering wheel,
girl strung from a tree.

Reached by summer,
and unafraid of after.

A Position

In the city, I carried my nothing, we were both so tired.
My nothing grew smog for wings.

Told a friend about the end of the world,
but she had a small child.

How quickly a piece of paper gets to be fire.

She told me I need to have hope.
I have nothing but hope.

I know the unrelenting blue does not concern me.

Mojave Roulette

I still know joy.
Rooms I've wrecked, and rooms I've left so careful.
Hymn of the boyish hair and the golden limb.

Do you worry for me?

Butterflies killing
all pretty on my windshield.

Who can name this flower or cancer faster?

Syncope

Left with his knife, I can get
into certain bottles.

But this is the curl of the rose

where I'm going alone. One bat rots

midair; no other bats notice?
An earring

singing something awful
to an ear.

Snow Metal

And me, I like my blood.
Isolate drums

in and out of the avalanche-lilies.
Gathered in veins, it drifts.

Oilbirds and swiftlets, the sonar of prey.

And me, I like my blood.
Isolate drums

in and out of the avalanche-lilies.

Clustered broomrape. The sonar of prey.
Fucking glacial. *No music* I said.

Windflower

Bluster and veil,
my beautiful soldier

I told to come over, then hid.

Pretend we never met, my mouth could say

avoiding obvious
         comparison to flowers—

anemone/an enemy.

Driven from edgelands, waits.

Cinema Lake

Silver convict,
sometimes his back

could make me. Relentless,
that stroke of a highway—

snow and meat.

Lone

A room smelt of mildew, then him.
Of a blondish

persuasion——no need
to persuade

for nobody's trouble
or shoulders

are like anyone else's shoulders,
though I do think of golden hills

or a fire on a list of all fires,

and the angel of *I can't remember*,
face down on the bed.

The Field, and the Knower of the Field

It's still raining those perfect pills
in the town

where he turned me over.

A strange contentedness to death,
her perfect concealments.

Beretta in the console, like it knew.

Conspiracy Theories

The butterflies hate me. The ones that come
at night that think they're moths—

the largesse and the fathom.

You're watching skies, they're crying blood—our gallery
of most persistent storms.

Eventually, I'll fall for something gentle.
No language

ever loved me back.

Temblor Range

So what if you thought that you knew me?
In the shadow of oilfields

bruised sea of scorpion weed, the land beyond
exhausted—.

The first time I thought of death
as a place that might help, I was only a child.

Later, I knelt for you, knowing that it wouldn't.
Some said that I needed God; in the soft light

and dreaming of atrocity, I took each snow-colored pill
the way I was told.

I could live here, I thought.
Only one tree in the whole of the valley.

THREE

(Wind became
my additional lover.)

What If the Invader is Beautiful

In the tallgrass
where all gold starts

wind became
my additional lover.

His hand the inflorescence
one finger partially gone—

Lovegrass/
Panicgrass/
Witchgrass/

**

I carefully researched
how to bait my trap.

Took the small blonde charmer
out of town.

Stealer of cholla,
eater of sun-murdered plants.

I knew it would die coming back.

**

Ajo lilies
now up to my waist.

What blackened
the opal knowledge—

What his ghost finger traced.

Hello, Panic, My Old Friend

Now a stranger
strokes my hair. Depraved

the swarm
of monarchs
in my chest—(anything en masse

is also terror.)

Ambulance man
has eyes like yours,

two ponds that kept
the mare alive

except for that one summer.

Erotic Transfer

Filmic, I thought
of my own silhouette.

To be urgent with silt,
whose origin is feldspar.

Under white cloth, your frantic
hand.

If grasses would anyway tremble.
If a shoreline we'd never deserve.

In a photo another man took,
intimists | in mists.

(Here, I want to leave a
damselfly, forgotten——). A room

of dodged perfume.

Tenderline

At first, just breathing was remote—
a series of tender isles

I'd know by dawn.

What is the purpose of skin?
To keep things out, and in, and yours

damp apricot lands
where even my sadness won't save me.

Assembling the agonists of fate,
each horse completes its winter.

Hell's Bells

Loneliest I've ever been is a rest stop outside Willcox,
Arizona, in a kill-wind, in my too-thin dress.

Beyond the blonde-shatter
dust of trucks, I stalked the hawk-moths

that haunted the
datura, told only her creamy petals

what I want. Delirium-ed secret:
even the moth

was stoned. When God puts blood on the road,
it looks nothing like its mammal.

Open Range

This is a book about joy.
The place where we'd lain

now thick with flowers, laced lightning
through the tenderness of drapes.

Today I learned of butterflies sequestering
milkweed's toxin.

Wild indigo
began her creamy sprawl. A train

derailed in a windflaw
and the fields on fire on purpose.

We counted cows,
especially the dying

giant bags of velvet
filled with God—

The Road is the Sickness and the Cure

In the truck, it was both of us crying—
admiring each other's method in the dark.

Once, I ate needles for love.
Pried the poison from the flower, and how

your moonlit kindness saved me.

In the long abandoned brothel
we stood near the heart-shaped hole

where the hot tub had been.
Red, I'll presume.

Implausible and finite as a rose.

Groundsmoke

Given a sagebrush-ed summer,
this barely a road

what aching is
led to this lake. I am here

and no longer
believe

any injury is imminent.
Season of fire, predictable sky-led wreckage.

Each fucking is still
a blazing star, untie

the halter at my neck
like a symptom.

Rangelands

The river curved
informed by something ancient.

A vital wound
drawn out between swept hills.

I could die out here tonight

owning nothing
but the knowledge that ravens will find me.

Doomed cattle out to the West.

Doomed in the hands
of the occupant grasses.

But the sky all church again.

Slip

Color of rabbitbrush. Palest
of unsung jonquils. Awoke

still warm in it. His ever
botanical touch.

Silk, so,
thank the spiders.

To be called to—
ornamental.

All the Arizona
grasslands.

His hands in it:
redundancy of nicotine and vice.

Destroying Angel

Beyond the universal veil
pitch perfect, emeraldine—.

The forest softly edged with fern delirium.

I thought my anger would be endless.
But nothing is endless.

The nothing is endless.

Larrea

Moved the jackrabbit
from the road, laid her under
a bush. Land of little

shade, we do what we can.

One sport is crying while driving.
Another the daffodil light.

All the mornings I've found you, been
found.

**

I'm just eating a sandwich with Sarah,
when the wind picks up, and her hair

becomes another,

crucial, planet. Night running off with
itself. Away

from your star. So soft
is the fur

of the currently—

Why Meadow

By Dying Lake, a damselfly lit in my hand.

Tender bones bleached bright in the animal wash— and
the sweet back of his neck after rain.

What we gave for this, and clearly would again.

The irises live for no one.
They die in the alkali meadow where they were born.

Mostly, they drink snowmelt. Sometimes rain.

Unpraised, we think, *and better for it.*
And, in doing so, we praise them.

Desire Path

The butterflies pull, oblivious to where

I wasn't willing. Wandering death-bird,
diminutive echo

of whence we had been gentle.
There was love, I'll give you that,

beneath the grass that seethed—
an endless viceroy affliction.

Now men design machines
that render love

obsolete—unless we won't
believe it. Take my hand.

What would you do with me
in the unimagined prairie.

Lucky

Dusk in the rift-valley now, saffroning.
Wild horses

reduced to spindle
skeletal trees—

The chestnut one barely an existence.

In the grimly lit adobe,
Amargosa

he holds me
like a storm-charm.

This is not
what I thought I would be.

Acknowledgments

Academy of American Poets *Poem-a-Day*, *Bear Review*, *Camas*, *Colorado Review*, *Copper Nickel*, *Cortland Review*, *Dreginald*, *Everyday Genius*, *Furious Pure*, *Gulf Coast*, *The Journal*, *Like Starlings*, *Luna Arcana*, *Manor House Quarterly*, *Schlaag*, *Tin House*, *Typo*, and *Zocolo Public Square*.

Thank you to everyone at Four Way Books, especially Martha Rhodes and Ryan Murphy, for your ongoing support of my work. I am very lucky.

During the ten years I was writing this book, I was buoyed by so many friends, kind acquaintances, and generous readers. I fear excluding anyone, please know how much I appreciate your support in all its forms.

For enduring friendship of the most soul-sustaining kind, thank you to Karyl Newman, Sarah Maclay and Chris Clarke.

Jeff Griffin, thank you for not only loving me, but truly seeing me. It means the world.

Notes

"Real Country Dark"—the title is a line from the script of Stanley Kubrick's *A Clockwork Orange*

"The Field and the Knower of the Field"—the title is from *The Bhagavad Gita*

"Hello, Panic, My Old Friend"—was influenced by and is in conversation with *Ars Poetica (cocoons)* by Dana Levin

"Larrea"—"land of little shade" a variation on Mary Austin's *Land of Little Rain*

"Lucky"—the phrase "storm-charm" is from Robert Macfarlane's *The Old Ways*

Select Locations

Spy Mountain 34.3311° N, 116.3983° W
Lavic 34.7466° N, 116.3752° W
Rangelands 42.32246 N, 106.30891W
Larrea 35.1234° N, 115.5204° W
Groundsmoke 37.6096° N, 118.7204° W
Lucky 36.3003° N, 116.4106° W
Erotic Transfer 37.8175544°N, 118.5775194°W
Temblor Range 35°19'25.877"N 119°47'48.469"W

About the Author

Louise Mathias was born in Bedford, England, and grew up in England and Los Angeles. She is the author of two full-length collections of poetry, *Lark Apprentice* (Winner of the New Issues Poetry Prize) and *The Traps* (Four Way Books), as well as a chapbook, *Above All Else, the Trembling Resembles a Forest*, which won the Burnside Review Chapbook Contest. For the past fifteen years, she has resided in Joshua Tree, California.

WE ARE ALSO GRATEFUL TO THOSE INDIVIDUALS WHO PARTICIPATED
IN OUR BUILD A BOOK PROGRAM. THEY ARE:

Anonymous (14), Robert Abrams, Debra Allbery, Nancy Allen,
Michael Ansara, Kathy Aponick, Jean Ball, Sally Ball, Jill Bialosky,
Sophie Cabot Black, Laurel Blossom, Tommye Blount, Karen and
David Blumenthal, Jonathan Blunk, Lee Briccetti, Jane Martha Brox,
Mary Lou Buschi, Anthony Cappo, Carla and Steven Carlson,
Robin Rosen Chang, Liza Charlesworth, Peter Coyote, Elinor Cramer,
Kwame Dawes, Michael Anna de Armas, Brian Komei Dempster,
Renko and Stuart Dempster, Matthew DeNichilo, Rosalynde Vas Dias,
Patrick Donnelly, Charles R. Douthat, Lynn Emanuel, Blas Falconer,
Laura Fjeld, Carolyn Forché, Helen Fremont and Donna Thagard,
Debra Gitterman, Dorothy Tapper Goldman, Alison Granucci,
Elizabeth T. Gray Jr., Naomi Guttman and Jonathan Meade,
Jeffrey Harrison, KT Herr, Carlie Hoffman, Melissa Hotchkiss,
Thomas and Autumn Howard, Catherine Hoyser, Elizabeth Jackson,
Linda Susan Jackson, Jessica Jacobs, Deborah Jonas-Walsh,
Jennifer Just, Voki Kalfayan, Maeve Kinkead, Victoria Korth,
David Lee and Jamila Trindle, Rodney Terich Leonard, Howard Levy,
Owen Lewis and Susan Ennis, Eve Linn, Matthew Lippman, Ralph and
Mary Ann Lowen, Maja Lukic, Neal Lulofs, Anthony Lyons,
Ricardo Alberto Maldonado, Trish Marshall, Donna Masini,
Deborah McAlister, Carol Moldaw, Michael and Nancy Murphy,
Kimberly Nunes, Matthew Olzmann and Vivee Francis,
Veronica Patterson, Patrick Phillips, Robert Pinsky, Megan Pinto,
Kevin Prufer, Anna Duke Reach, Paula Rhodes, Yoana Setzer,
James Shalek, Soraya Shalforoosh, Peggy Shinner, Joan Silber,
Jane Simon, Debra Spark, Donna Spruijt-Metz, Arlene Stang,
Page Hill Starzinger, Catherine Stearns, Yerra Sugarman, Arthur Sze,
Laurence Tancredi, Marjorie and Lew Tesser, Peter Turchi,
Connie Voisine, Susan Walton, Martha Webster and Robert Fuentes,
Calvin Wei, Allison Benis White, Lauren Yaffe, and Rolf Yngve.